# How babies grow

Bobbie Neate and Susan Henry

This book tells you how babies change from helpless, tiny infants to toddlers who can do many things for themselves.

You do not have to read the book from beginning to end. Just turn to the pages that interest you.

**Contents**

# A newborn baby

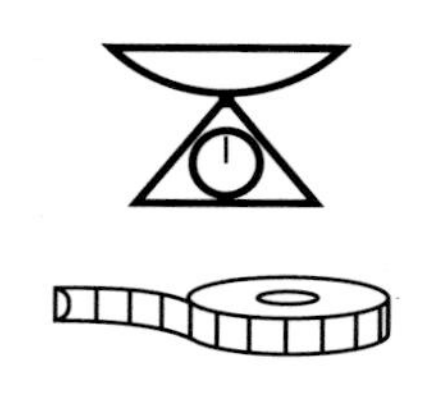

| weighs | 3½ kgs |
| --- | --- |
| measures | 53 cms |

**When babies are born they are very small. They need milk to help them grow.**

**Newborn babies are not all the same size.**

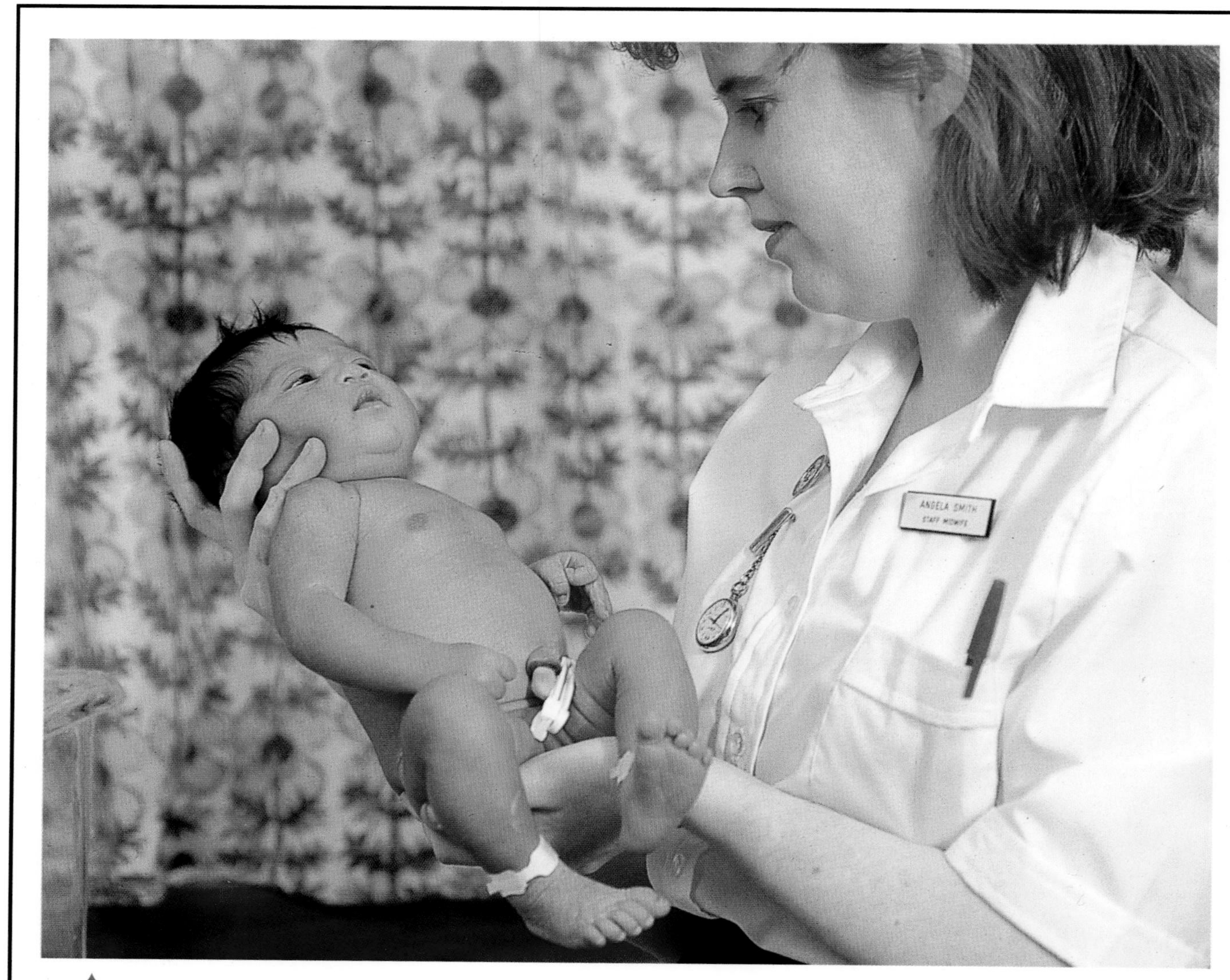


This baby has just been born. She is 1 day old.

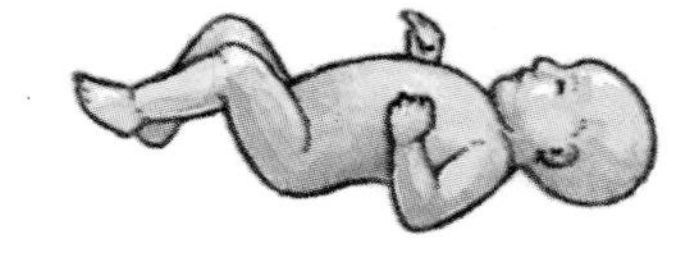



newborn

The baby gets milk from her mummy's breast or from a bottle. She sucks the milk in the night as well as in the day. The milk helps the baby's body to grow. Every bit of the baby gets bigger as she grows both inside and outside.

First the baby will have milk from one breast then she will suck from the other.

2 years

## A newborn baby

**All young babies need to have their heads held. This is because their neck muscles are not strong.**

Newborn babies like to be wrapped up and held firmly.

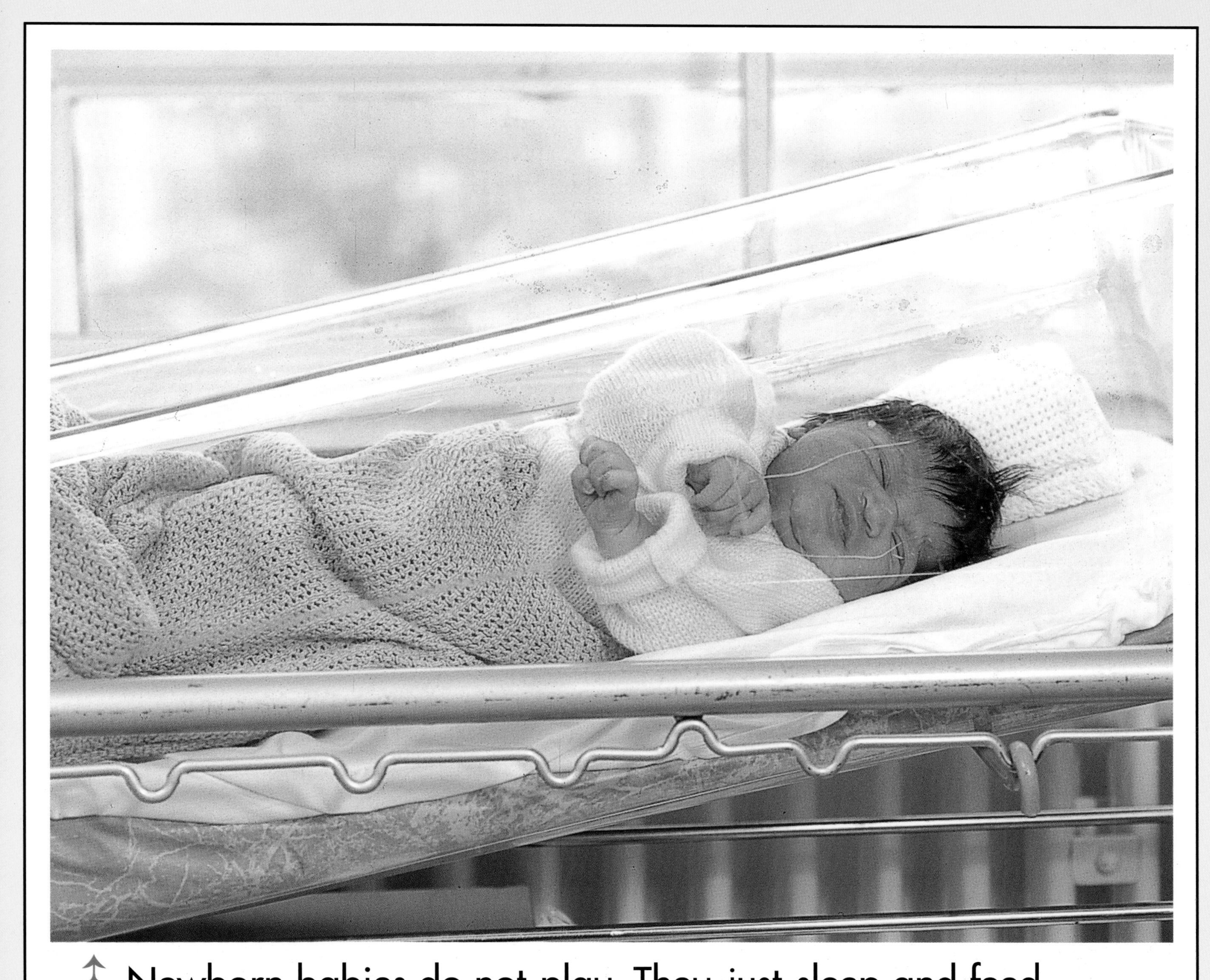

Newborn babies do not play. They just sleep and feed.

## Nicola

Nicola cannot hold her head up herself, but she can see things and she can hear. She can grip things too. Newborn babies cry to get adults' attention. They also cry if they are hungry or if they have a wet nappy.

# A six week old baby

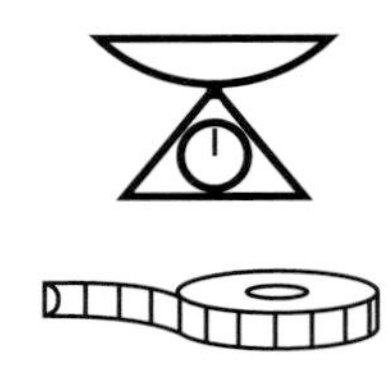

| weighs | 4 kgs |
|---|---|
| measures | 55 cms |

**When babies are about 6 weeks old they start to smile.**
**They do not really play but they love to look at brightly coloured things.**
**They still have milk for food.**

Six-week-old babies are very interested in human faces.

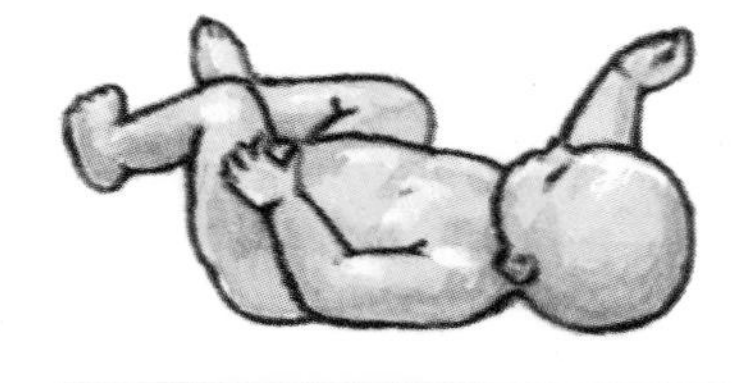

# David

David is 6 weeks old. He has changed since he was born.
He now smiles at the people who talk to him.
He is now old enough to stay awake to look around him.
He likes to watch people most of all.

Some six-week-old babies stay awake for 1 hour.
Others stay awake for 5 minutes.

2 years

# A three month old baby

## (13 weeks old)

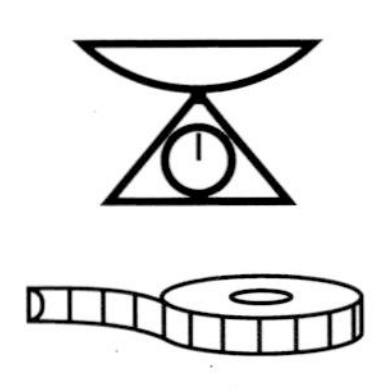

| weighs | 6 kgs |
|---|---|
| measures | 60 cms |

**When babies are three months old they can start to have solid food. This is often called baby food.**

**Young babies still need lots of milk because they are growing fast.**

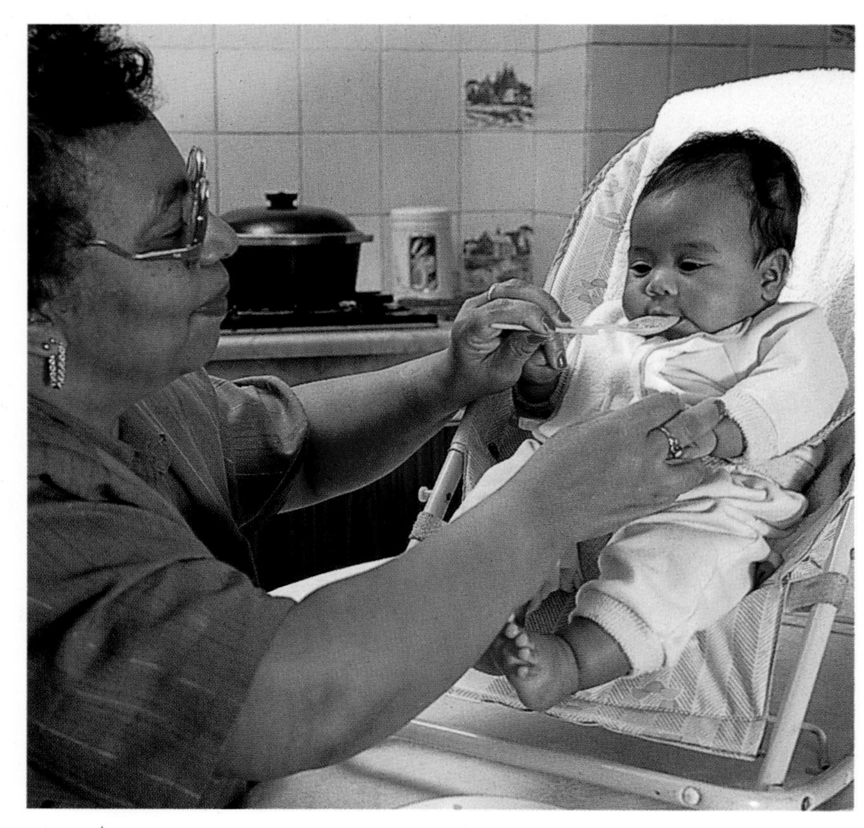

Baby foods must be very smooth and runny.

3 months

Babies' first solid food is usually a sort of porridge. Later they can have mashed up fruit and vegetables as well.

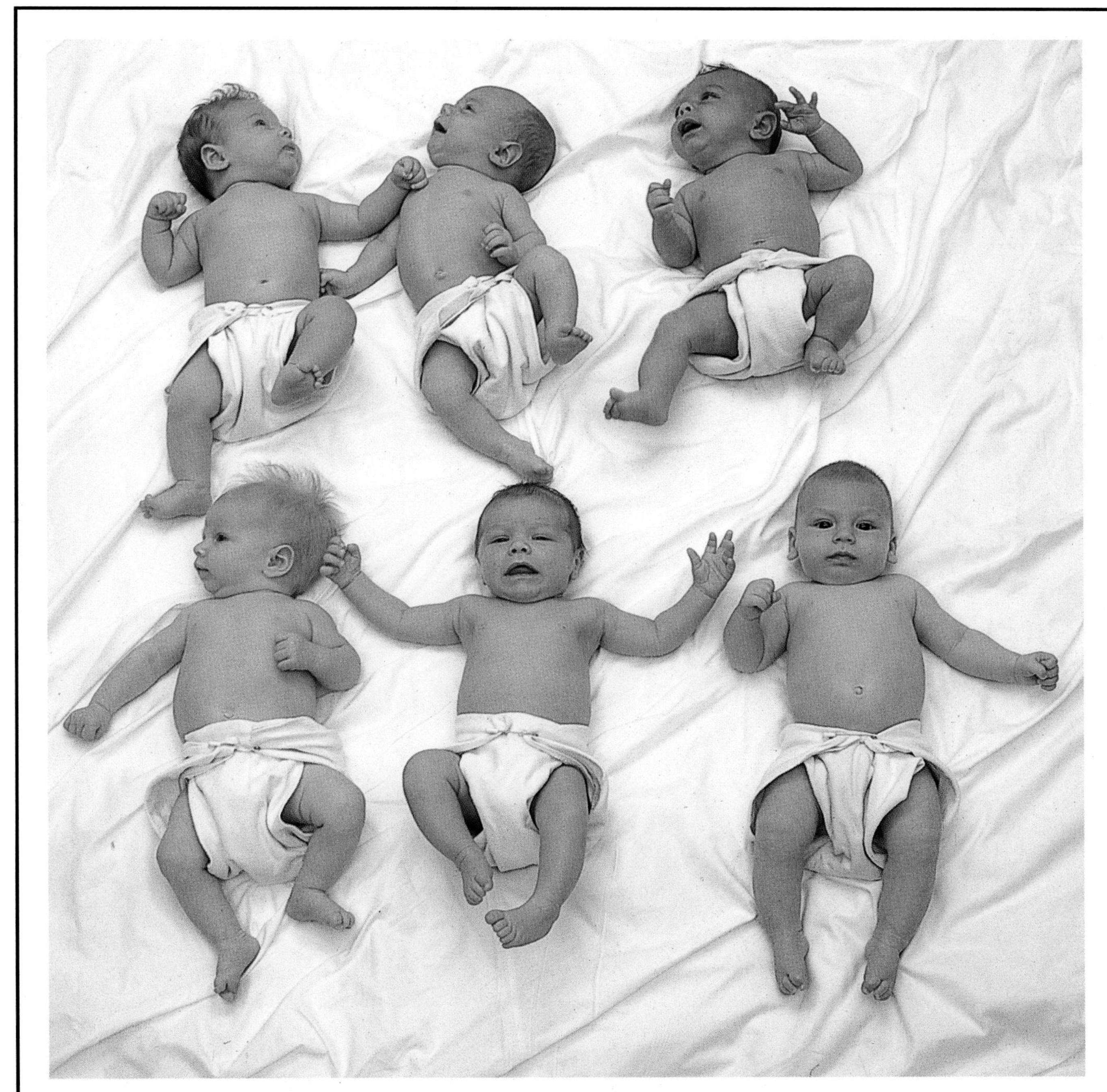

These babies are not the same size. They are all 14 weeks old.

Some babies grow faster than others.
Babies and children have growth spurts.
A growth spurt is when they grow very quickly.
At other times they grow much more slowly.

2 years

## A three month old baby

**Three-month-old babies do not sleep all day. Most days they stay awake long enough to play with their toys. They like to play with rattles.**

This baby enjoys kicking without her clothes on.

## Tunay

Tunay is learning all the time. He watches and learns. He still cannot sit up on his own but he can now roll over from his back to his front.
It will not be long before he can crawl.

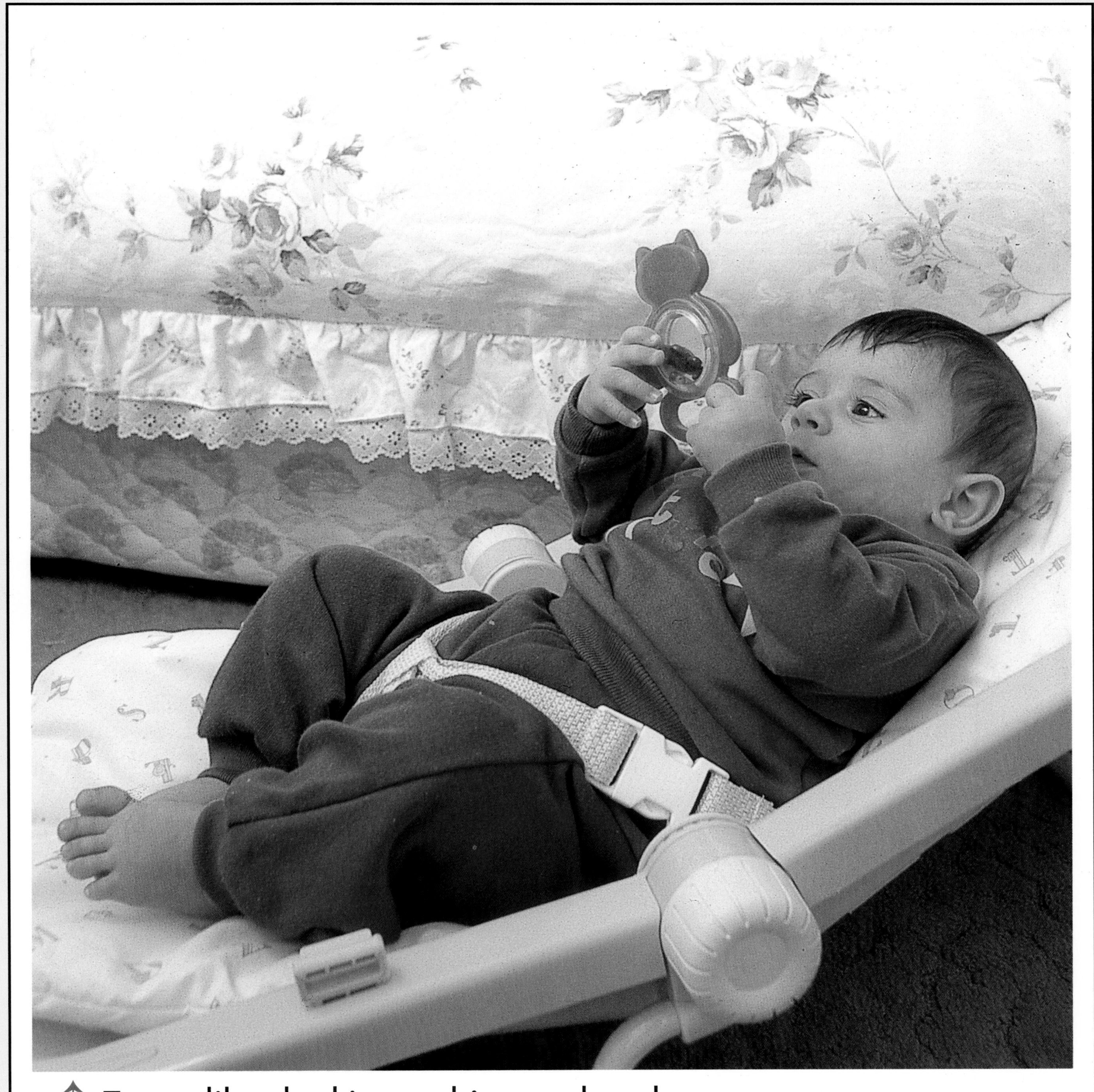

Tunay likes looking at his own hands.

# A six month old baby

## (26 weeks old)

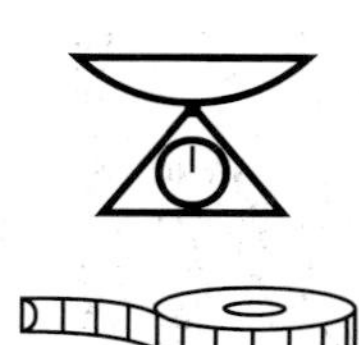

| | |
|---|---|
| weighs | 8 kgs |
| measures | 68 cms |

**A six-month-old baby has three meals a day. He can now eat hard things as well as soft food. He still needs lots of milk each day.**

Some six month old babies have their milk from a trainer cup.

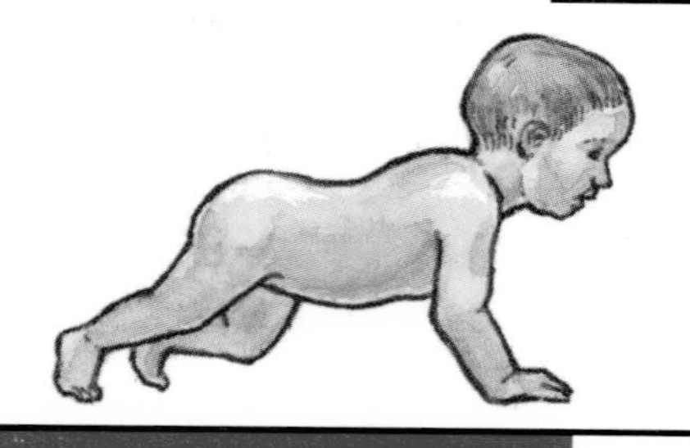



6 months

## Paul

Paul is six months old. He has got his first two teeth. They are in the middle of his bottom gum. He likes to chew on hard food like toast, pieces of apple and carrot.

Some babies get their teeth earlier than six months and some babies do not get them until much later.

2 years

**Six month old babies need less sleep than younger babies. They can now stay awake to play.**

## Paul

Paul can sit up and he loves to play with toys.
He likes to put things in his mouth to taste them, and to feel whether they are hard or soft.

Paul cannot talk but he makes lots of noises that sound like real words.
He understands some words that his family uses.
When he is about 9 months old he will say his first word.

Paul can crawl. Sometimes he pulls himself up and tries to talk to his daddy.

# A one year old baby

## (52 weeks old)

| weighs | 9½ kgs |
|---|---|
| measures | 72 cms |

**When babies are older they need meat, fish, eggs, cheese, fruit and vegetables. Milk is not so important now.**

## Mai Ling

Mai Ling is one year old. She has three meals a day with her family and she can eat the same food as her older brothers and sisters.

Her food is usually mashed up but she now has five teeth so she can eat some hard foods.

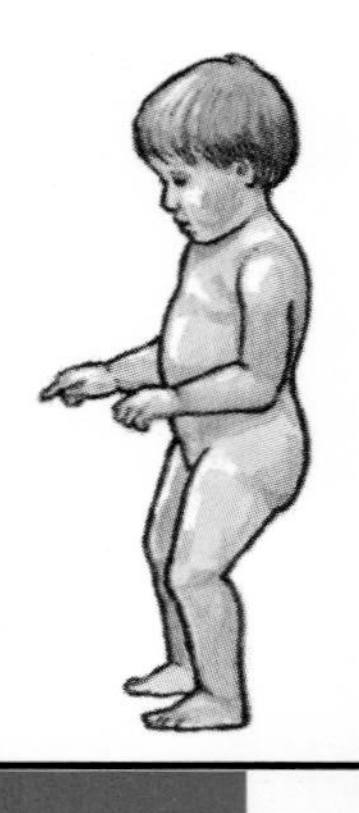



1 year

Mai Ling still likes a bottle of milk at night.

2 years

## A one year old baby

**Most one year old babies can crawl.
Some one year olds can walk too,
but they are very unsteady on their legs.**

One year old babies do not know what is dangerous.

Mai Ling can play by herself but she likes mum or dad to be near.

## Mai Ling

Mai Ling can walk ten steps.
She can now pick up small things
with her thumb and finger.
She can also pull toys along with a string.
She can even scribble with a pencil.
She can say ten real words and
she understands lots of words.

# A two year old toddler

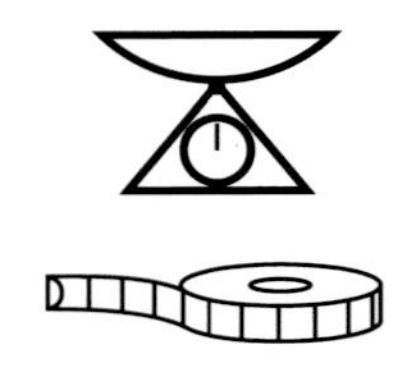

| weighs | 13 kgs |
| --- | --- |
| measures | 86 cms |

**Most two year olds can talk, walk and run.**

**They can use a potty.**

This two year old can feed herself.

## Gareth

Gareth is not a baby any more. He is a toddler. Toddlers often have bad temper tantrums. They get cross when they can't do things that older children do.

Gareth is learning as he plays with his toys.

2 years

Use this chart to find out when a baby learns to walk and talk.

## How a baby develops

| | Newborn | 6 weeks | 3 months | 6 months | one year | two years |
|---|---|---|---|---|---|---|
| **Physical Development** | | smiles | rolls over | crawls a little<br>sits up | crawling<br>walking a little | walks steadily<br>runs |
| **Play** | | looks at bright objects | can hold rattles | likes to drop toys | plays with simple toys | plays with many toys |
| **Language Development** | cries | gurgles<br>cries | coos – coo-coo<br>laughs | babbles<br>bababa<br>dadada | first word<br>mama | says two words together<br>dada gone |
| **Food** | only milk | only milk | a very little baby food<br>lots of milk | finger foods<br>soft foods<br>milk | mashed up, meat, fish eggs, cheese | family meals cut up into pieces |

# Glossary of words used in this book

**Attention**
You get attention when somebody is taking notice of you.
Babies like somebody to play with them.
This is getting attention.

**Breast**
A breast is a part of a woman's body.
Mothers of young babies have milk in their breast.

**Crawl**
Crawling is moving on your hands and knees.

**Muscles**
Muscles are the parts of the body which help us to move.
A baby's muscles get stronger as they get bigger.

**Scribble**
Scribble is a child's first writing.

**Temper tantrums**
A temper tantrum is when a child gets very angry and will not do what he or she is told.

**Trainer cup**
A trainer cup helps babies learn how to drink from an ordinary cup.

# Index